This book belongs to

_____

I0354699

This book is dedicated to my children - Mikey, Kobe, and Jojo.

Copyright © 2024 Grow Grit Press LLC. All rights reserved. No part of this book may be reproduced in any form without permission in writing from the publisher. Please send bulk order requests to info@ninjalifehacks.tv

Paperback ISBN: 978-1-63731-869-0
Hardcover ISBN: 978-1-63731-871-3
eBook ISBN: 978-1-63731-870-6

Printed and bound in the USA.
NinjaLifeHacks.tv

Ninja Life Hacks®
by Mary Nhin

ELEFANT

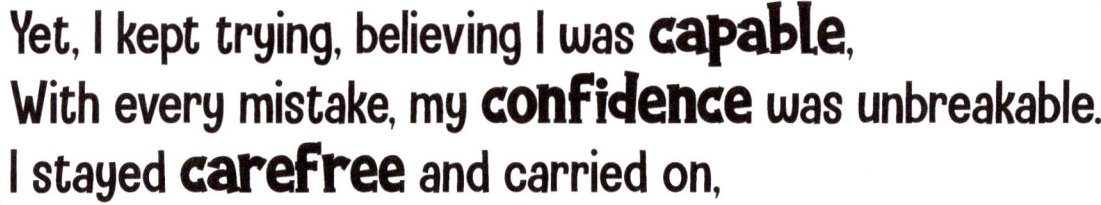

The colors swirled, the room a mess,
"Oh dear," I thought, in a little distress.
But before I could panic, what did I find?
The machine made magic of a different kind!

With each little glitch, the machine lent a hand,
Turning frowns into smiles in a magical land.
It taught me that mistakes aren't so grim,
They're lessons to learn with triumph within.

But then came a day, a challenge so great,
The machine stuttered, its gears spun in wait.
For a moment, I panicked, what could I do?
Without my dear machine, how could I push through?

So if you spill or trip and fall,
Remember me, Gritty Ninja, and all.
Mistakes aren't scary, that's for sure,
They might unlock a hidden door!

The end of my tale is quite clear,
I turned mistakes into confidence, oh dear!
So go on now, give it a try,
Embrace your oops, reach for the sky!

I was inspired to write this story after I realized that failing is my expertise.

We invested a lot of money into two restaurants, but they failed.

The first year I founded my educational company, Grow Grit Press, I invested over $250,000 and failed.

Sometimes, it's hard for me to be a patient parent. I get upset too quickly and sometimes I'm too harsh. During these parenting moments, I fail.

When it comes to health goals, I try to eat healthy and exercise most days, but I falter.

My husband and I used to argue a lot.

I fail a lot and am so used to failing, now I joke that it's my job. One thing I've learned is that I learn by trial and error. Today, we have a five location sushi chain and an educational company that is my love and passion. My husband and I just celebrated our 27th anniversary. I'm used to dusting off my pants, getting back up and trying again. I'm an expert at that.

Mary Nhin

Check out lesson plans that contain fun activities to support the social, emotional lesson in this story at ninjalifehacks.tv!

I love to hear from my readers.
Write to me at info@ninjalifehacks.tv or send me mail at:

Mary Nhin
6608 N Western Avenue #1166
Oklahoma City, OK 73116

 @marynhin @officialninjalifehacks
#NinjaLifeHacks

 Ninja Life Hacks

 Mary Nhin   Ninja Life Hacks

 @officialninjalifehacks

www.ingramcontent.com/pod-product-compliance
Lightning Source LLC
Chambersburg PA
CBHW041522070526
44585CB00002B/42